Errant

Gabriel Levin was born in France and grew up in the United States and Israel. *Errant* is his sixth collection of poetry. He has translated from the Hebrew, Arabic, and French and has published a collection of essays, *The Dune's Twisted Edge: Travels in the Levant*. He lives in Jerusalem.

By the same author

GABRIEL LEVIN

Errant

CARCANET

Acknowledgements

Grateful acknowledgements to the follow journals in which some of the poems were originally published: *PN Review*, *Raritan* and *Stand*.

The epigraph is taken from Giordano Bruno, *On The Heroic Frenzies*, a translation of *De gli eroici furori* by Ingrid D. Rowland, text edited by Eugenio Canone, the Da Ponte Italian Library, published in collaboration with the UCLA Centre for Medieval and Renaissance Studies, University of Toronto Press, Toronto, Buffalo, London, 2013, p.205.

First published in Great Britain in 2018 by
Carcanet Press Ltd
Alliance House, 30 Cross Street
Manchester M2 7AQ
www.carcanet.co.uk

A CIP catalogue record for this book is available from the British Library.
ISBN 978 1 78410 634 8

The publisher acknowledges financial assistance from Arts Council England.

Typeset in England by XL Publishing Services, Exmouth
Printed and bound in England by SRP Ltd, Exeter

Contents

Cicada: Let us go, and as we walk discover whether or not we can unravel this riddle.

Tansillo: Very well.

Giordano Bruno, *On the Heroic Frenzies*

At the fourth watch extend
  your blank errancy
your slip away rills of light, oh my cilia
  bright dawn, my cloven
hoofed, tawny Aurora

rising from your flushed bed
  of noughts, O my new-
born fleeting doe, my occluded, errant
  one, spun tremulous
on your spindly axis

Obsidian

Pressure flaked, crested
blades, dark, amorphous – with no crystalline
structure to speak of – ridged

debris, strung along the shoreline
in gleaming ribbons where
water scours

the lithified volcanic ash
and the shored-up, three-masted Barbarossa
points the way up

to the old quarry deposits,
crosshatched in drab prickly burnet sleeping
the summer months away.

I've pocketed the knapped
mineral, smooth, lustrous as the Theotokos
in her silver-plated

armour with only the face
exposed to the halting gaze – and lips – under
the pendulant, low

wattage in the oil lamps – how
your light probes inly, my little, glassy nodule
my core, my fracture.

Alba I

Qu'ieu vey l'alba e-l jorn clar

When she kicked off the comforter
and tugged the window open, a querulous
flock of scavengers crash-landed en mass
in the neighbour's yard.
                          He rolled on his side
to shut out the racket and groped back
to the vacant scenery, though soon enough
they'd upped and gone
                          and staked their ground
further afield – the gray-hooded ones.
There's no telling what was lost in waking
with no one left in the clear day.

Reading Nasir-i Khusraw

for Eric Ormsby

Between plum and cherry tree a tourbillion
of gnats: winged, predicative, a slipknot
of twilit ciphers. The garden holds untold
promises as I step over acrid cat-droppings raked
into baby mounds to peer at the dwarf
princess lilies. Jurjani solicits manifest tokens
of the tacit world, and you,

                      O subtle expositor,
proffer *Kan!* (Be), delighting in the fruit
trees planted in tubs on the Cairene rooftops.

    How the seven lights burnish the under-
leaves, while the bulbul (here I go again) blurts out, 'Begot,
begot, begot.' In this land of unlikely likenesses
I like to think of you reconciled to the multiple,
the one-by-one natty raking-in of joys, no-see-ums
nipping at my earlobes with a vengeance.

*

Why this measure of dust and water, darkness
and light wherever your peregrinations
bear you along? The moon bobs up like a gourd
over the Haram – jot it down in your diary,
876 leagues away from home, east of the great river –
its light acts like water *moistening the dry
parable with the dew of sense.*

                    Floats over Silwan
in a pinafore. Like the Sodom apple it dusts
the valley with its smoke and ashes. Pale fruitage.

First rains pelt the yard in due season,
even the midges scramble for cover
as I fetch back indoors your Twin Wisdoms,
lest the shower smudge its pages, between reason
and revelation, muffled fireworks, and from the foot
of the mount neither cloud nor quaking.

Atropos

The fowl of the air deadeyes its prey in ever-tightening
circles, while you brush by us with your bobbins

and threads. *Snip. Snip-snip.* Risen from some finer dust
than ashes. Cumbrous, for all your airs.

★

With one jab of the clawing machine down comes
the edifice, crash crumbling around its ghosted

tenants: intact, unaccounted for: toasting
each other – if only they had voices – across the pit

rock-drill, bone-meal, no skin off our back, thick
as thieves in the fallout, *ho-ho, hosanna in the highest.*

★

I'd watched from my perch the burdened
lorries churning up the ramp, and felt the circle tightening

and on the hilltop Ice Palace the skaters knocked
against the railing, and knocked again in their turnings.

The Shoulder of Hinnom

1

When the skies clear I can hear the secreted
birds fidgeting in the forked pine branches blurred
in the puddle, and behind me a long, straggling line
is leaving the white brick Mandate cinema –
the lives they'd seized on rushing past them shine
in their eyes as they make for their cars,
key-rings at the ready: and the Sabbath siren

goes off even as the rains leave off, and with a shudder
of their feathers the birds forsake the air.
It doesn't seem fair walking these precious few steps
to look on over the shoulder of the wadi,
the raindrops off the streetlamps sending off
sparks across the watershed, Sultan's Pool inked in,
small finds coming to light when the skies clear.

2

The wadi beds drain their small
finds where the creviced
cyclamen hoards its flame: one twisted
nail, bottle-caps mistaken
for coins, toe-pried and tossed
into the nettles, not the grit-brushed
galloping griffin signet, go on
then, skirt the burial shafts, past Thigh-
bone's Edge, following the rockface
veining, eyes peeled for what
the rains might leave encrypted
in Hinnom's lap,

a pair of high wire, gray
hooded crows have you covered
(wouldn't you know it) this side
of Gehenna, keep walking
as they watch your back, round
the bend, past the mudslide,
button-eyed marigolds under the ruined
barrel vault, not the spindled
glass, nor the rolled-up fiche-size
benediction in beaten silver,
but sutured skies over potter's field,
the almond trunk

lashed to the overhang
won't bale you out, torn blossoms
on the gravel path, crushed
bird's mandible, not the verdigris
cache, cist or hollow for fibula
or alabaster dish, but a scraping
wind where the scarp sheers
and scraps of litter swirl round
your feet, open-air fiend,
what's that stuck to the thorn bush?
Mke hs fce shn upn
us, Selah.

Think back on the little threshing floor:
how the east winds stung as the chaff
fell and scored the crinkled soil on the orphaned
hill, and the thrashing in the mulberry
leaves stirred the heart so, and the young ran
through the breaches when the shadow
figures scaled the wall, scarcely more

real than the tales clocked at nightfall:
lay down, lay down your doll-eyed charms
as the cock crows – Gallicantus! – and brings
the house down. Lame and blind, imagine
how the scales dropped from our eyes like sheaves
to the sickle's stroke, and light poured
into the clearing where we held our ground,
clairvoyant as the salvos shook the mount.

Alba II

Tugging at the blinds she caught
sight (so she thought) of a flurry-tailed
thing that shot out from under
the pickup
       though there was no
telling in such a place – foreign
to all accounts – and only *he* knew
what had been wrought
               to the form
stunned under the wheels a life-
time ago, how the thing fought
in the mind for air, and died.

Hellas

i.m. S.H.

How it dips its feathered oar in the slipstream
as we're ferried across the straits, latching its eye
on an airy morsel tossed from the deck and snatched
in its crackerjack bill. One last sidelong
glance – fore and aft – and it veers off from the wake
the ferry churns swinging round to dock.
It's a toss-up which way to turn once we've found
our land legs. Unscrambling the signs

gets us only so far. Can't we just knock about
the place a bit? *Have a heart.* A room, a bed,
a meal to chase away the fumes from the crossing.
The House of Proclus couldn't have stood
far with its abraded reliefs – you know the sort:
hands drawn in filial grief, barley cake offerings,
a serpent lured out of its omega coil sips
at a foaming bowl. Dew of the vine.

After Avraham Ibn Ezra

(1092–1167)

My coat's a sieve to sift barley or wheat.
I spread it over me taut as a tent in the pitch dark.
How the astral bodies shine in defeat!

From within I spy Selene on her beat,
the Pleiades, and haloed Orion making his mark.
My coat's a sieve to sift barley or wheat.

I'm fed up tallying in rain or sleet
its chinks, jagged as saw-toothed gashes in bark.
How the astral bodies shine in defeat.

No thread can hope to patch up indiscreet
rents and gaps in the weave, unworthy of remark.
My coat's a sieve to sift barley or wheat.

A fly coming to rest its stringy feet
on my coat will surely regret dropping in on a lark.
How the astral bodies shine in defeat!

O God, in exchange for these tatters treat
me to a robe of glory, customized, nothing too stark.
My coat's a sieve to sift barley or wheat.
How the astral bodies shine in defeat.

What Drew Me On

for Tamara Rikman

1. The Vision of Er

What drew me on in my own faltering
summoned in due time to rise from the damp meadow

the journey begun? The unfolding ambit a whiplash
of looping paths, quick vanishing sightlines

I knew not whether earth or air cushioned my walk
and plodded on, but whose words – 'the stars shine

through the holes of my cloak when I spread it out in the pitch
dark of night for shelter' – had wandered

into my mind, the future more vivid (if true
I shall be humbled) a sieve to sift wheat

or barley, while on either side scratchmarks, indigo dimples
beckoned, and I thought I saw a canister

floating above me like an asteroid, or was it a trapezoid?
Stenciled shapes, charcoal fisheyes, a column

of light, more radiant, purer than cloud-borne Iris spanned
the heavens and plunged to the sea-floor

★

Get a move on, I told myself
as iridescent light blebs
rained on the lime-
washed field, the slant, stippled
plane, cutting a paper
trail, dark, snaking footpaths
for one lately snatched
from the pyre, unfettered

setting out to a place
of forks and windings
chalkline byways, groundless
vistas – 'with no thread
to mend its gaps' – once again
lines flung back at me
from light years away

I, Er, of the tribe
of Everyman, lately revived,
am cradled in a ark
of unborn song, swaddled
in my overcoat: 'Oh god
won't you exchange it
for a robe of glory?'

★

Gazing up after another day's crossing
I beheld light beams fastened like a ship's undergirders

that kept the constellations from dispersing
where the Spindle stretched from bottommost heights

and all the orbits rotated on their axes
'How so?' I shook my head, chalking the tongue-tied

wonder with a free hand, peeling the coalface
skyways back, 'How so?' hook and staff darkly

lucent, the huge whorl, hollowed and scooped
enfolded, one hoop nesting within another

airbrushed, spangled, changing gears, in reverse
orbit to the Spindle that spun on the knees

of Necessity, and a Siren leaned over the rim of each orb
releasing one sound, one note as the spheres

whirled in concord with the Fates, Necessity's daughters – Spin
Twist, and Sever – singing of what was, is, and will be ...

2. *Again Placing the Patterns*

Who would have believed your return.
The terraqueous globe ringed in florescent green –
but there you are, making fresh tracks

on the still wet ground, dappled
with anticipation, casting your lot with the wind-buffeted
silver bush (Calocephalus!), the diamond

frost, the wavering stem of the wand flower
paying out, winding you in, dawn lifting the urban
drek around you in its rubbery arms

sticking its sticky fingers into bills raw
with song, dawn walking you through the Way
of Seeming as you rub your eyes

and fix your gaze on the ruinous
splendor taking hold of the dangling, aerial
roots sucking at light dawning

*

These are the materials

to construct your inflammable

bark and hoist the shroud

of being: paper, scissors

stone – Weigh anchor! My bantam

weight anima, my feathery tres-

passer – off you go now

over ignitable, rag paper seas

of fancy – how many knots

have you chalked up, akimbo, atilt

afore mast, my tangled, runaway

shadow on your maiden voyage

(every voyage a maiden)

Stone. Paper. Scissors. Sing

★

when you lie down
and when you rise up from the bed
of leek green and rapeseed
of red hibiscus and slaked lime

whiting, of Tyrian dyes
secreted by sea snails – *argaman*
and *tekhelet* – when you lie
down and rise up, unpicking the blue

from the white, the sun
at its zenith, and the sea's polished
mirrors leveling the city
on its mounds, and you behold neither

sun, nor sea, nor mirror
nor anything other than them.

★

I wasn't familiar with the Hebrew
for rhombus and heard
threatened

                    rather than suit of diamonds
                    when you spoke of
                    its emergence, the words

barely
distinguishable in my ears, but hadn't it none-
the-less suited us,

            to speak of the need
            to ward off the slant, nagging
            threat of losing
            it?

though I wish I could say where *it* lodged,
tucked under the temporal
lobe?

The pituitary gland?
                        Hai ben Yaqzan –
the Living Son

            of the Wakeful – surmised
            what ever once occupied the cavity
            of the heart

he'd removed   from the dead doe
who had nurtured him was It,

('where had it gone,

through which outlet
of the body had it taken leave?')
   Did you know

            rhombus once stood as well
            for a whirring
            string instrument
            used in

the ancient mystery cults
called in its day
a bull-roarer?

> Might we have come
> a full circle, did the oblique
> figure portend more

than meets the eye?

★

Again placing the patterns of life on the ground before us
(this is Er speaking) far more numerous than I might have imagined

how were we to read the lots flung at our feet? How choose
from the sundry shapes, free hand cut-outs: what lives, what tyrannies

what strange, earthly comminglings; penuries, riches, whether whole
or atomized
lives stunned to a standstill, and those that kept running on ...

stared back at us with mimic force. Had I been there, or not? Every-
man. Winged out-of-the-body, I'd watched my betters

draw their lots. Swan. Nightingale. Lion. Eagle. Ape. And the wiliest
of them all, alighting on Nobody lying in some forsaken

corner and minding his own business, told the poor fellow
he alone had been chosen to step into his skin.

It's a hazardous business choosing a new life. Keeping your eyes
fixed on the just calling, undaunted by the undisclosed

brushing against the daily, unfinished spectacle, for it will save us
if only we believe it, and we shall safely cross over.

3. Bel Imago

First came sooty beings shinning up walls
    gulls on the look out low-circling the grotto
    off port Levanzo, the Paleolithic shoals –

then came the potter's shard, the calcined logo
    life cycle spindly sparring partners, crooked up
    or flat out, sow and reap, and ready to go –

then came the hand-coiled, fretted drinking cup
    the gift, the barter, the lingua franca
    celebrants, rounding the cape in festive getup –

then came the wheel-made Lady of Phyla-
    kopi, tubular priestess in polychrome
    O unearthed bel Imago, bel Alpha –

then came (under the hippopotamus) full blown
    in the papyrus thicket a little man with straw
    blond, sticky hair, punting his reed boat home –

then came winged gigantism, leonine maw
    or else the kilted procession, minuscule frieze
    on the cylinder seal, part of the jigsaw –

then came Kouros stepping into the light breeze
    on the road to Thebes, dimpled under-lip
    softly beveled in a smile meant to please –

*

then came birds to peck at will-o'-the-wisp
     grapes clustered on the plate, uncanny likeness
     for the famished, before spitting out the pips –

then came tall tales apace on a broad canvas
     in manifold drafts where anything goes
     (see how they dash into the arms of trespass) –

then came bawdy scenarios, household curios
     the reading of bridal mysteries below hot
     thinly smoking fumaroles as the cock crows –

then came aureate Byzantium, shot
     through with semblances, ivory caskets, vellum
     and tesserae, all is *theosis,* or else naught –

then came the arabesque in rapid-sum
     defile, out of Arabia curling round the heart
     of every dome its calligraphic rerum –

then came the stonemason wheeling his cart
     of grotesqueries, grimace of faces under
     the weight of a capital, rent apart –

then came silent vows, and nothing (sweet plunder
     of faith in Assisi, preaching to the bird-
     covey of little sisters) short of wonder –

then came portraiture in full dress, spurred
     on to strip the heart bare, the dark surround, glaze
     upon glaze probing the gaze, undeterred –

★

then came a window onto a prospect, haze
    lifting over cypress and stream, and deep within
    a birth foretold, the betrothed in a daze –

then came the Campagna, a rustic inn
    sunlight washing over the nut-brown broken-
    down aqueduct, taking the long view in –

then came costumes, Odalisques, token
    charms, a blotchy palette soaking up the bustle
    in the souk, as tonalities beckon –

then came the plein-air ramblers to rustle
    up the show, chemistry kit for a paint box
    sunburst and vapor in atmospheric tussle –

then came the toss up: how outfox
    the rule of thumb as the eye beat a path
    across the abrupt divide, pine and rock –

then came the sleepwalkers: in wrath
    tearing down the scenery, and opening wide
    their mouth and eating all they found to the last –

then came belle Imago once more with the tide
    lapping full fathom as she put forth
    her phantom hands and said: paint the dark side.

4. *Light Years*

Shake, press down, watch color appear.
Hadn't I read in Benjamin how parables bud
into a blossom like the margosa outside your window
or unfold like a paper boat into a flat sheet
of paper, to smooth out and decipher
in the palm of your hand? The margosa
with its bitter bark, though now it's the steadfast

almond blossom palming off its knaps and petals
on the road to the coastal plain – shake, press
down, and watch color appear, read the instructions
 in small print, but when you pick up your terra
cotta marker, it's not like you're asking 'What does
the man behind them mean, the one who blows
the trumpet?' or, 'Why all the citations

anyway, don't you have a mind of your own?'
A snarl in the traffic I can't see the end of
drives me out of the bus crawling down Ibn Gabirol
and onto the street: if you strip away the scenery,
one prop at a time, what's left for the eye
to latch onto? I loop around the mover's van
blocking the sidewalk, sidestep a bulging carton

crayoned Handle With Care: nothing, it's like
the inside lining – Benjamin again – on the nether
side of that 'nothingness,' feeling my way
around the furniture, I recognize the neighborhood
by now, the park, the kiosk, and, yes, a scatter
of margosa trees and in the distance the tapering
casuarinas we're always mistaking for pine,

it too imported from the subcontinent, when
would that have been? Prussian, cerulean
baby blue, an ever-errant azure, a Jonah-thrive-
and-perish-in-a-day blue, is it any wonder
your precursors clambered up drab, unlit
stairwells with their portable easels to take in
the rooftop view, light needling the solar

reflectors, bouncing off the mounted water
tanks, and hadn't it been the same with you, no
sooner back in town , you'd found a poky
rooftop shack, and, undeterred by the *vroom*
of the jumbo jets low-flying overhead, scrawled
SUMMER IN TA arched over the sleeping
figure scribbled in black and just a daub of yellow.

The girl etched in the rays of the midday sun
in a billowing dress swinging on a trapeze outside
a turreted, walled city (circa '65), is back
in her natal city, built on soft, red *hamra* soil.
And it's not like you're asking, 'Are those wings
etched into the copper plate? And is that the head
of a dog in the right-hand corner?' as you shake

press down, and watch color appear from the tip
of the jumbo, garden craft marker, and the possibility
of a new clarity hangs in the air where a child leaps
once, twice, thrice, to grasp the hairs of an air root
dangling out of reach as I cut across the park, the point
is beside the point, a little to the left, dark dwindling
to a vanishing point beyond which the city

encrypted a hundredfold, stages its own vanishing
act, folds into itself, blossom to bud, in reverse
slow motion, and the garden paths unspool
in the concourse of the mind, and there you are
two flights up, the streetlamps lighting up the margosa –
purged by fire before descrying the stratosphere
and Ibn Ezra's cloak hardly bearing the weight

of a fly, through which the stars pulse, recall
your own charting of the heavens with drawn blinds
and swift, random strokes in our sublunary world.
Light years, light years! Gauging the distances, how
your body tracks the stark, emerging shapes down
slanting without mercy from nowhere, and the line
whirls you round as you enter the current.

Snow in C Sharp Minor

Perhaps I too shall write
a little research in snow
as you did (when was it, '75
in NY?), moderately sober in my house
slippers in the East

and since neither prophecy
nor reward brings the sapling fruit
tree to its knees, I must slip outdoors and shake
its powdery sleeves free

of the lightest of encumbrances

then waddle-hop between boot
track sink-holes back in, bright flakes
evanescing in the chill
night air – slow, but not too slow
in a singing style

perhaps I too am a snowed-
upon islet in Jerusalem, snapping out of it
to shut the rattling window,
as if all possibilities for pampering
had been – but aren't these

your words? – sealed off.

Someone Knocks at the Door

for Zali Gurevitch

And my mother looks through the peephole and announces, Brenner is here. אֵין לִי כֹּחַ בִּשְׁבִילוֹ [I don't have the strength to deal with him] *I call back from my armchair.* This is not Z's dream but his mother's, which she recounted to her son on the phone the other day and which Z now relates to me over coffee at the Smadar where we've come to mark the occasion of his early retirement from the university. Today he'd taught his last class and partied with his students who had passed around ice-cream cones.

*

We're pushing sixty and inevitably the conversation revolves around age. A friend tells Z that old age is the square root of your present age multiplied by ten. When you're nine, thirty seems old; when twenty-five, fifty. But I'm struck by Z's mother's dream. She's eighty-five, which is old for us. When not fretting over our own ailments, we attend to the decline of our parents. And yet the dream speaks otherwise. This morning, upon waking, Z's mother's dream returned to occupy my thoughts. I myself had dreamt plentifully, but as soon as I'd kicked off the sheets whatever dreams I'd had receded from memory, as though making room for Z's mother's dream.

*

My first thought had been that Z's mother had dreamt her son's dream. Perhaps in old age we become the transmitter of other people's dreams. For I cannot help seeing her in the role of the intermediary, the go-between between her son Z and the great Hebrew writer Haim Yosef Brenner who comes knocking at their door. Why Brenner? Ashkenazi Hebrew for 'burner', the name apparently stuck to the descendants of a distiller of spirits. Brenner's own father, however, eked out a living in the small Ukrainian town of Novymlini as a *melamed* or traditional Hebrew schoolteacher.

Unvocalized we get four hard consonants – b-r-n-r – in which one of the letters is duplicated. *Bet resh nun resh*. A sort of Ur-sound, like in H.N. Bialik's essay 'Revealment and Concealment in Language:' 'Then a kind of savage sound burst spontaneously from his lips – let us assume, in imitation of nature – resembling a beast's roar, a sound close to the *r … r* to be found in words for thunder in many languages.'

★

In a sense Brenner *was* a distiller of spirits: of Hebrew, and of his own anguished soul. He arrived in Palestine and stuck it out – unlike his compatriot U.N. Gnessin, who wrote the first Hebrew roman fleuve and after touring the fledgling colony in 1908, beat a hasty retreat back to Russia; Brenner held his ground in what was at the time an impoverished outpost of the Ottoman Empire. In spite of it all. He bore the troubles of the land on his back with the same stubborn persistence that he'd lugged copies of his short-lived literary journal *HaMe'orer* (The Awakener) in a sack slung over his shoulders in London's East End where he'd sought refuge after deserting the ranks of the Czar's army during the Russo-Japanese war. That would have been in 1905, the year of the October Revolution in Russia. In 1907, in one of *HaMe'orer's* last issues, appeared a translation of Oscar Wilde's play *Salome*. Two years later he landed penniless in Palestine. *Breakdown and Bereavement*. The title speaks for itself. The first modern Hebrew novel written in Palestine was unsparing in its portrayal of life in the *Yishuv*, the colony. And yet for Z's mother's generation Brenner loomed larger than life. She was born, after all, only two years after Brenner was killed defending a homestead outside Jaffa from Arab rioters during the May Day disturbances of 1921.

★

Brenner was 'the new Hebrew narrator of our age,' as Bialik would say, he was the Originator, the conscience of the Second Wave of Immigration, who'd shed all the accouterments of the Diaspora in coming to Palestine 'as a man longing for the sun,' and who increasingly took on the role of ascetic and vagabond, tramping the length and breadth of the land, teaching Hebrew to Russian immigrants in the small Jewish farming settlements. Squinting through the peephole of Z's apartment door his mother might have been impressed by 'A short man with a full blond beard and beautiful blue eyes,' which is how S.Y. Agnon describes Brenner in *Only Yesterday*, his own novel of the Jewish colony in Ottoman Palestine, dropping in on friends in the then new neighborhood of Neve Tzedek – today a fifteen minute walk from Z's home: 'His movements are informal and his clothes are threadbare, and he is bashful among people. Such reticence isn't because people are held in such high esteem in his eyes, but because he thinks little of himself. But his wisdom shined forth from within his bashfulness without ever exceeding his innocence.'

*

'A mother cannot but help thinking of her child as remaining forever in his prime,' Z shrugs his shoulders, running his fingers through his gray-peppered beard. 'For her Brenner and I were – are – of the same age.' Z's mother has summoned up a meeting between kindred souls. With a touch of hyperbole one might say that for a short while all that separates the brooding, saintly figure of Brenner and the author of the hyper-contemporary, bluesy collection *Double Click* is a door in a Tel Aviv apartment and a mother's solicitousness. The question remains: why does Z wave Brenner away. *Ain lee koach beshvilo.* In the course of our conversation Z speaks of his father's mental deterioration. They may have to hire a Philippine carer as his mother *has no strength left for him*. The same words again. Z's father, whom I remember as a robust water engineer, was orphaned of his father – struck dead by Cossacks – as an infant in Russia and grew up in Mandate Palestine, imbibing the pioneer ethos, singing Russian melodies and declaiming Bialik's poems around the campfire.

*

So whose dream are we talking of? Or perhaps we should ask: for whom was the dream intended? If solely for Z's mother's, one might say that her son voices her own exasperation, her helplessness as she peers through the peephole at the spent glory of her past. Should she let in the image of youthful virility, whether spouse, lover, or poet of the State-in-the-making (and I now recall Z boasting on more than one occasion how the poet Haim – *Haim* – Gouri had tugged at his mother's braids in kindergarten) or not? Dreams complete themselves in the telling. Z's mother rises from bed and calls her son. Hello? Z: Yes? I've had the strangest dream. *Nu?* Guess who appeared in my dream? *Nu?* Someone knocks at the door and I look through the peephole and lo and behold Brenner is standing there on the other side. You're kidding. Honestly. Haim Yosef Brenner? That's right. So then what happens? I call out to you, Z, Brenner is here to see you, and you call back from the armchair at the far end of the room, *ain lee koah beshvilo.* There is a long pause. I snubbed Brenner? Yes, dear, he stood there on the other side of the peephole for a while with those soulful eyes of his and then left.

★

We share a world when we are awake; each sleeper is in a world of his own (Heraclitus). We can never know for sure what Z's mother dreamt. In each telling and retelling the dream undergoes its own transformations in the teller's and the listener's mind. Yet I would like to believe that Z's mother was not so much telling her dream as handing it back – redirecting it – to her son, like a letter slipped into the wrong mailbox. In another dream of Z's mother that Z recounts to me that same afternoon, of which I remember only a fragment, someone exchanges shoes with Z. So perhaps this is what is going on, Z's mother gets to walk in her son's dream, where the latter has no time for Brenner. Idiomatically speaking *ain lee koah beshvilo* would be more like, I just don't have the patience for the man anymore. And all of this is conveyed, or rather boomed from the son's armchair across the living room to his mother.

★

To interpret the dream as a family romance in its senescence, mother and son shutting off doddering father from their cozy habitat, seems pat, even though I've hinted as much earlier on. No, I'd rather like to suggest that Z is turning away from Brenner himself, the man and his shadow: the mood swings, the soul-searching and self-torment, the *yetosh* (bug), as Beilin writes in his memoir *Brenner in London*, that ate at Brenner's heart, and of course life's high drama lived out in the throes of a catastrophic era: the pogroms, the October Revolution, the Yiddish-Hebrew war of languages, World War I, the jostling for power within the Zionist movement, an oppressive, poorhouse Palestine. Is it not possible that Z is asking (in the name of Hebrew literature?) for a reprieve? Leave me alone Brenner, leave *us* alone: we've had enough of the Fate of the Jewish People. Let me be. Let me shuffle to my study in my advanced years (as old as the state, Brenner) from where I can look out at the rooftops of Tel Aviv to write my 'Blues for Lunch':

Solfigetto for whiskers
Prelude for pestering
Ragtime for palpitations
Symphony for mounting anxiety

Suite for a complicated grief
Impromptu for a birthday
Sonata for clarity
Rock for strong things

Bebop for a shower
Con brio for a cup of tea
Pianissimo for a door
Blues for lunch

2008

And Cush

begat Nimrod, the first man of might
on earth. His torso polished

as a dry riverbed, the hawk
on his shoulder, cushioning his ear

with its feathers, wired to his killer
instinct. Hadn't we looked up to the legendary

figure until we ourselves coarsened
into his double? – Now prowess

gives way to slyness, and Nubian
sandstone abrades into plaster, jute, tin

and fiberglass, while another bird perches
on your shoulder, its beak buried

in its ruff. Dream on, prowling your old
stomping grounds for easy prey.

'To Each His Chimera'

In Camera (1948)

Poking your head out of the window
you catch sight of the porters from Saloniki

directly below, leaning over the bars of their empty
carts, far from home, with nothing to show

for their labors, while the shadows of nameless
passers-by cross the street – it will take

a millisecond for the shutter to slake
its thirst on the anonymous

scene, but the *click* of the Leica brought
from Berlin pleases you, and you fancy the hooded

lady in black crepe has stepped out of the Grimm
Brothers into sunny Palestine, fraught

with its own grim tales, the uprooted
arriving, and taking leave, as you duck back in.

Body Politic

The face askew in deadpan
dread at its own reflection, eyes
sunk in their sockets, deploying anti-
personnel flechettes in a conical
arch where affections once held sway:
at sixty-five you could say attrition

you could say, been there; memory
overtaxed, punch drunk with one déjà
vu after another, fists spoiling
for a fight, oh my confederate, bosom
companion, blood count off
the charts, where do we go from here?

Pastoral

How I love the sound of the Palestine sunbird
chip-chip-chip, followed by the gargled cooing
of unseen doves and the sight of white cabbage
butterflies over the wand flowers – our lives
brim over with the commonplace: clods loosened
where the pitchfork lies by the wall, nosy bees
in the rosemary, and, hey, wouldn't it all be just
fine if not for the new breed of mosquitos
bloodletting at low altitudes? I flap the covers
of Lamentations shut, Smack! Gotcha. *Abroad
the sword bereaveth.* What else awaits the avid
reader this morning? The Brutality of Fact,
and, peeking under the pile, yesterday's ungainly
exhibition catalogue: Let's Have Another War.

Study for a Portrait

after Francis Bacon

Is that your adversary pinned
down, on edge, the dangling yellow wattage

casting its own gloom over the dubious
object of your gaze? It won't take

more than a sitting or two, maybe three, before
the trapped face is squashed

and scrambled into a form of – how did
you put it? – exhilarated despair.

Sometimes you're happy whipping a rag
across the figure impregnated

with color. Violence beguiles. But what lies
behind the ruined composure if not

more ruin? The walls collapse, the vanquished
stares back at you from the rubble.

Echo

*Hell*o, anyone there? Scraped knees, lips caked
with cinder dust, while my ear cocked to the gap
seizes on the faintest scrap, 'Aren't you a sight
for sore eyes,' I dimly hear coughed up, *sore eyes!*

After Simonides

It is Danae borne over the sea and bemoaning her fate
                                        Dionysius of Halicarnassus

        ... Seeing how
within the ingeniously carved
chest violent gusts
and churning waters struck
her with dread, not without moist
cheeks she cuddled Perseus in her loving arms
and said, ' – Child, how I suffer

while you sleep, tender
suckle-hearted, napping in the bolted
crate, cheerlessly launched
on the   unlit night
and indigo murk, oblivious
to the spray cresting over your head
and the snarling winds
all bundled up in your purple-dyed
bunting, such an adorable
face – had you felt endangered
by the engulfing danger
surely you'd prick up your tiny ear
to my words

listen then: sleep, my newborn
babe, and let the sea sleep
and our innumerable hardships
sleep, and you, father Zeus, show forth
some sea change, and be easy
on me if my appeal seems overbold
or anything but just.'

Death of a Cinéaste I

Abbas Kiarostami
1940–2016

Hold the line! He makes a zigzagging dash
for higher ground as the voice keeps breaking up
on him and the Land Rover skids to a stop
by a scatter of walnut trees: the lens picking off a rash
    of unmarked, upright stones – *Hello! Hello!* –
before panning to the radiant highland
across the plain, while the stranger's far too stand-
offish, cradling his mobile, to mellow
at the scenery.
                    Scraps of song
drift within earshot; zoom in, follow him round
as he tracks the Persian air to a ditch; but
whoever's down there holds his tongue – *Hey, what's wrong
why d'you stop?* he shouts into the hollow ground
catching midair a femur in reply. Cut.

P*aR*D*eS*

for Ardyn Halter

1

The volts in the flex, oh mystère, fluoresce
as I step back, on the watch for what lies
behind the frames stacked upright at the far end
of the revamped coop, borne as a glazier
might stretch out his arms to lug one unwieldy glass
pane at a time, 150cm × 150cm,
not exactly your own beanpole height, but
close enough. Leaning further back, you pivot
the canvas round for closer inspection

where you've given your brush leave
to roam in thin, indeterminate strokes along
the fluted columns surging up in recessed
spiral symmetry – memory's slit, salamander eyes,
casting sidelong glances under
the porticos, flicker at the show-through
ambulatory, then dilate as vitreous
free-floating recollections, submerged
in their paradisal sac, summon you

2

back to Shiraz, Zoroastrian nights,
the Rav thrashing you with spring onions
when you recite the Plagues (a young Englishman
abroad on the eve of the Shah's flight) circumambient
orchards, rose gardens wherever you trawl
your gaze; but of the four who entered – will I ever
get it right ? – only one went up whole
and came down whole: 'Arriving at
the stones of pure marble, don't say, Water,

44

water!' And when you scrambled up
the crazed bricks for a better look, the wall
buckled under your feet. Unscathed
you circled back to the night prayer hall,
Shabestan, auriferous in the failing
light – reprised in the long view's ad hoc slide
rule, now and again, Masjid-e
Vakil, hovers in ticker tape celestial blues,
in volumetric flourishes of your brush.

3

Of the four who entered Pardes
one peered and perished ('Then his torch faded
and the gates opened – and he fell head
over heels, alongside a smoking brand, on the brink
of the void') while folly brushed
another at a glance, as it is written: keep your fingers
out of the honeypot! But you poked
around the premises, squinting at the candy-
colored tilework, swollen-headed cupolas

resting on their laurels, and hunkered
down to copy the patterns, a lanky
apprentice to the virtues of the illusionist's art,
if ever there was such a thing, 'vestibule
after vestibule – and where was the last
gate? And where the banquet hall?'
Here then, now then, cooped in
your coign of vantage, all is enkindled,
brindled, stroke by freighted stroke

all is a gibbous lunar disc, or beckoning
telescopic lens, rounding the corner…
Of the four who entered I imagine
Elisha ben Abuya, aka Acher, stealing
into Sa'adi's *Gulistan*, dazzled
(but hadn't he cut the shoots?), decrypting
the cheeky bulbuls' gibberish
in their green pulpits – was any renegade
dearer to the Sages? Accosted on

a Sabbath by a wench on the road, he tore
a radish from its bed and gave it to her,
and she said: He is an Other. And he: *I have already*
heard from behind the veil. – Step up,
step up and back, for yet an other stab
at getting it right this time. The high vaulted
ceiling crumbles at your touch
and re-assembles, nacreous, opalescent,
viridian, for the final rendezvous.

Death of a Cinéaste II

Chantal Akerman
1950–2015

With the blinds lowered, legions of motes break rank
through the slats, and the camera – your standby
stand-in – rolls; your errant Private Eye
locks onto the rooftop terrace across a street named for the thank-
less Jonah the Prophet. The recorder picks
up the heavy scuffle of your heels in the stowaway
rental – your temporary digs;

                          the shuffle & clack of the stray
specter you've turned into, clean out of tricks
how to stay afloat, while the film rolls on
an eternity before you set up your proxy against the pane
and random bursts of street-life rend the air
winnow the quickened from the lately gone
the rooftop looming large, reconfigured, a couple in plain
sight – your voice breaking in, already elsewhere.

Outtakes for Ritsos

Convalescing

The shadow on his lungs had a way
of turning up at the oddest hours, there was always
a smash up somewhere to take in
the fallout suited him fine – what the doctors cured
he'd take back with a sharp intake
of breath, his pen shadowing him at a safe

distance, and when a ban was placed on his words
he rolled them like tabac and licked
the gum seal-tight, the mix he smoked in the near-dark
letting the words glow for a moment
as he watched the locals heft on their shoulders
their bait baskets, like the years

The Swimming Lesson

The parcel wasn't getting any lighter
as he rounded the corner, he fancied plunging off
the pier, the gift held close

to his chest as he went under
like the father who'd leapt, his child wailing
in his arms before bobbing up
doing the dog paddle.

Didn't they say the museum? The string cut
into his fingers. Surely they'd be waiting
for him at the appointed hour.

À La Tour Abolie

You couldn't tell ruins from boulders
nor boulders from goats nor
whether scratch-marks stood for swallows
or gallows, and there weren't any signs
of foul play on the plate fished out of the water.

I don't know, he said, 'the inner economy

of such a man's life would present
a monstrous picture.' The spooked olive
trunk is nobody's fool, its stricken
limbs chiming with the general
sentiment that the drowning reflection
in the mirror was more to your liking.

Twice Removed

Startled awake he paced the room in a sweat
lifted the lid of the cheap music box whose jingle
sounded meekly to his ears. I'll have no truck
with you, he said to the ballerina whose leg

had snapped like a wishbone. To make matters
worse, the lowering clouds over the far side
of the bay were club-wielding shadow-puppets
behind a propped-up sheet. Then he woke.

Tin Star

He'd sit there under
the carob, the makeshift firing-range
too close for comfort

mistaking the knob-
headed, bleached asphodel stalks littering
the field in the failing

light for half-notes
stricken from their staves,
while the bright

thing in the heavens
could have belonged to the only
sheriff in town.

In the Taverna

The owner and his buddies had their heads
turned to the game. That's before Dawn
gave notice. You can kiss your dreams goodbye
she said, leaving her name scrawled
in rouge for him to wake up to.

Insomnia

The mosquitos were relentless, so he buried his head under the
pillow and composed in his mind the perfect sentence, in which
words vanished the moment their successor appeared; this was, in
effect, the essence of parole, not to be confused with parole, as in:
having served his sentence the malefactor went on parole (buzz off!
he told the bloodsuckers at his ears).

The Paring
for Nina Bogin

There's another way of looking at it
she said, wresting from him the paring knife.
Here, he said, handing her his gloves
which she'd wear to her liking inside out

feeling on her skin the paring he'd made.
Here too the dark pressed in on them
as they listened to the prickly artichoke hearts
fall into the bucket, one heart at a time.

Threnos

Omens are like that, a tray crashes
to the floor, a bird trapped in the lightwell

tussles with its shadow, and the body
diminishes with each blow dealt

even as the living image – I quote from
my betters – endures: it slumbers

when limbs spring into action, and bestirs
itself in sleep, in unaccountable dreams …

Alba III

'Scientia
holding the lamp, driven by doubt'
Robert Duncan

Count on the birds to leak
the news out in unctuous, sputtering cries
as she jerked the curtains apart
and the ruse dawned on her,
                              Ai, ai, ai, faded
the syllables that had once
quickened – enthralled to a voice. He woke
to her scalding stupefaction,

unmanned. Was it beastly of him to run
from the light? Heavens, what became
of the feckless pair?
                    Misrule at my shoulder
knows the score: Go on, turn the page.

'As Light Makes Both Itself And Darkness Plain'

Suppose we spoke
   of the sad passions –
the diminished

note in the mouthpiece
   drawn out, baffled intervals
of the inadequate

idea – days on end
   lime dust hung in the air
over the petrified

exteriors – unforeseen
   privations, the deferred
passage ending

in sadness: no point
   tracking the inverse image
the torqued starlings

provide – contours
   shifting in waterlogged
skies might have led

us elsewhere – say joy
   say credulity as the dog star
fixed in its heavenly

constellation links up
   with its counter-
part, howling at the runaway

moon, sprung loose
   from the Dead Sea, risible
over the ramparts

*

hilltop neighborhoods ignite
    into a myriad of flares
in the disparaging

eye, how it delights
    in the disconsolate, toying
with their contrary

natures: fear *risen*
    from the image despair
of a doubtful thing

remorse – while the hooked
    perennial elbows
out of the cracked

mortar, unfurling
    its twisted lobes
in deadbeat

February, limp
    stalks unbend, chin-up
over cordate

leaves in shiftless
    winter light, say cell
sap, tuber and seed-

leaf – say stick-
    by-me time-released
incarnates

*

but tell us, blessed
    Benedictus how a singular
thing, in as much

as it alone dwells
    in the mind
remains an object

of wonder for
    the unabashedly joyful –
while doubt

reigns over the impregnable
    knot in the solar
plexus, the chanted

incipits cut short
    in the foliage insofar
as a singular

inconsolable sadness
    grips the mind: such are
the affections

divvied up in the crackling
    air, such the crack-
downs in the civic

body – the spoil
    and recoil of the inner
most self – *say it*

then, and play it back
    so long as it is
of the essence

★

herba-alba , sticky
   essence of wormwood leaf crushed
between thumb

and index, flourishing
   in the abandoned grounds of
the Leper Colony

midsummer, snooping
   around its skirts, where the Aleppo
pines are just so far

from keeling over
   wind-licked outcroppings
a boulder to sit

in its shadow, this side
   of the aridity line, and reckon
what might become

of the better part
   of ourselves, in as much
as – how your pet

rider rings
   its changes! – *in as much
in so far* as there dawns

an image in the mind
   of renewal, where easterly
winds shake the pod

free of its seeds
   and even the gourd perishes
in a night

          ★

and revives – here
　　then where the crests of the receding
hills drift

south, balk at the sheer
　　drop to the salt
pans, I fancied the essence

of our ghostly selves
　　borne between the banks
of the dry riverbeds

spun like tumble-
　　weed in the warm currents
of air, from which

we take our origins
　　Creatrix on the brink
of creation

and under cover
　　of the derelict asylum
the adequate

idea, the promissory
　　note, wrung out of the hot
wind, is late

in coming, and the bell
　　tower, scumbled
on the horizon

might as well be
　　a crow's nest, for we flounder
far above the sunken

sea, and the blanched
   fig tree lists in the undertow
of its unknowing

and for want
   of reason, the city riffs
on its own undoing

★

time to be up
   and going, surely you're home
pacing – or stock still

I hadn't noticed
   the clump of squills
sprung overnight

with the slenderest
   of inflorescence ascending
the stalk, clear

distinct, in the fallow
   field, and the rains still ahead
of us – I'll be slipping

back daily, for certain, as a fresh set
   of flowers threads
its way up

they take us back a ways
   don't they? *Each thing, in so far
as it is in itself*

(geophytes, hadn't I once
   noted? secure in their sub-
terranean world)

persists in its own being
    calling up our own neophyte
days, Look! you'd cried

alighting on the tapering
    squill by the wayside, glossed
in my ear as the promise

before vanishing altogether.

Follow at a clipped pace the dry
   course tossing and turning in its gravel
bed, under the hair-trigger
   moon – Oh my pale insomniac
my sickle stricken beam

Hesperus is Phosphorus
   rounding the arena, under the last over-
pass, how the white, astral
   heat slants down its nugatory
fierceness on the defunct

line that once cut the village
   in two – you might have leaned out
the window to pick the prickly
   pears from no-man's-maw, if not
for the postings, Beware

Notes

The Shoulder of Hinnom. A shortened and slightly altered version of the Priestly Benediction: 'The Lord bless thee and keep thee: the Lord make his face shine upon thee and make be gracious unto thee: The Lord lift up his countenance upon thee and give thee peace' (Numbers 6:24-26), inscribed on a minuscule, rolled up silver scroll and dating to the mid-seventh century BC, was uncovered, during excavations in the late nineteen seventies, among a hoard of ancient artifacts in a row of burial caves just west of the Old City walls of Jerusalem above the valley of Hinnom and facing Mount Zion, the biblical site of the Jebusite fortifications conquered by King David (see I Samuel 5: 6–10). *Mke hs fce shn upn us* intend to convey in English the gaps and consonantal grouping of the Hebrew benediction. Vowel points written beneath the Hebrew letters were only added to biblical texts between the 7th and 11th century AD.

After Avraham Ibn Ezra. Born in Tudela, Ibn Ezra wrote secular and liturgical verse, but also distinguished himself as a grammarian, mathematician, astrologist, and biblical commentator. In 1140 he fled Spain in the wake of the Almohad conquest of Andalusia, leading the penurious life of an itinerant, wandering from one country to another – Italy, Provence, Northern France, England – and in the process introducing Hebrew, Arabo-Andalusian quantitative verse in Italy, which would become the new center of Hebrew writing. Ibn Ezra's secular poems are distinctly personal for the times, laced, as it were, with own brand of self-irony and humor. I have taken the liberty of turning into a villanelle the fourteen-lined, monorhymed poem attributed to Ibn Ezra.

*P*aR*D*eS*. *Pshat* (plain)*Raz* (hinted) *Drash* (homiletic) *Sod* (secret): the fourfold exegesis of the Bible. The acronym in Hebrew means orchard, *pardes;* Arabic, *firdaus;* stemming from Old Iranian, *pairi.daêza,* and the Greek, *paradeisos* for an enclosed park – 'to make (a wall) around' – from which is drawn the English word paradise. The parable of the four who entered Pardes appears in the Talmud Bavli tractate *Hagigah.* Legends concerning the renegade sage Elisha ben Abuya Acher (Other) abound in the Talmudic literature. Lines in quotes in section 3 are from the Hebrew poet H.N. Bialik's poem *'Hetzitz va-Met'* ('Looked Asquint and Died') written in 1916 and itself a modern-day exegesis of the Talmudic parable.